Genesis Talavera
Cristel Maradiaga
Carlos Mendoza Jacomino

Surveillance and the panopticon in the digital age

Genesis Talavera
Cristel Maradiaga
Carlos Mendoza Jacomino

Surveillance and the panopticon in the digital age

From a physical conception to a ubiquitous practice in the digital environment

ScienciaScripts

Imprint

Cover image: www.ingimage.com

This book is a translation from the original published under ISBN 978-620-2-16084-1.

Publisher:
Sciencia Scripts
is a trademark of
Dodo Books Indian Ocean Ltd. and OmniScriptum S.R.L publishing group

120 High Road, East Finchley, London, N2 9ED, United Kingdom
Str. Armeneasca 28/1, office 1, Chisinau MD-2012, Republic of Moldova, Europe
Managing Directors: Ieva Konstantinova, Victoria Ursu
info@omniscriptum.com

Printed at: see last page
ISBN: 978-620-8-63266-3

Knowledge is the only space of freedom of being'.

-Michel Foucault.

Acknowledgments

We would like to express our most sincere gratitude to all the people who made this book possible. First of all, we thank our families for their unconditional support and for believing in us throughout this process. Their patience, love and motivation have kept us going, even in the most challenging moments. A special thanks to our pets Pololo and Blue for being present in the creation of this book. To our mothers Wendy and Marjorie, who have always been by our side showing us their unconditional support and love. To our friends, who have been a constant source of inspiration, feedback and support. Thank you for sharing your thoughts and supporting us every step of the way in the creation of this book, every word from you was important to give us the strength to move forward with this project and put Parkinson's law into practice in an academic way. Your opinions and constructive criticism have enriched our work and helped us grow.

In addition, we extend our gratitude to our teacher Carlos Mendoza Jacomino, who taught us to appreciate writing, to develop our voices and to expand our knowledge without hesitation. His wisdom and guidance have left a lasting imprint on our path as future professionals.

Last but not least, we thank our readers in advance. We hope that what we are sharing in this book will be to your liking and inspire you to learn and research as much as it inspired us.

With gratitude,

Genesis Talavera and Cristel Maradiaga.

Table of Contents

Foreword

In the digital era, the notion of surveillance has taken on new dimensions, becoming a pervasive phenomenon that permeates all aspects of daily life. From the rise of social networks to the proliferation of connected devices, the ability to observe and analyze human behavior has evolved beyond traditional boundaries. The concept of the panopticon, formulated by Jeremy Bentham and fine-tuned by Michael Foucault, offers a valuable theoretical framework for understanding contemporary reality. On its face, the panopticon represents a control structure in which individuals are constantly observed, which affects their behavior, and ultimately, their identity.

In this context, digital surveillance manifests itself not only through data collection, but also through self-surveillance induced by interaction with digital platforms. Users, aware of being watched, adjust their behavior to align with social expectations, generating a cycle of control that perpetuates normativity. As technology advances, the line between surveillance and participation becomes blurred, raising crucial questions about privacy, autonomy and identity construction in an increasingly interconnected world.

This book seeks to explore how the concept of the panopticon is applied in today's digital surveillance, considering its ethical and social implications, as well as its impact on the way individuals perceive themselves and others. Through this reflection, it aims to offer an in-depth understanding of how digital surveillance not only affects individual behavior, but also reconfigures the dynamics of power in modern society.

Chapter 1: Origins of the Panopticon: From Bentham to Foucault

According to Gutiérrez Zurdo (2019), the panopticon was born from wanting to reform prison architecture, it was prior to Bentham. The precursors of this new architectural conception were architects with the idea of referencing the same circular architecture where the subjects are individually isolated in full light.

Bentham's idea of the panopticon was born as a result of a visit by his brother, Samuel Bentham, who subsequently ended up formulating and building the model applied to prison architecture which he refers to as 'Columbus' egg', and baptized as 'panopticon': from the Greek prefix Pan- (παν) meaning "totality" and the Greek word optic (οπτrκoς) meaning "the all-seeing eye".

The main idea of the panopticon was to find a way to solve the problems of surveillance through the approach that a single individual could watch everyone; the all-seeing eye as mentioned by Gutiérrez Zurdo (2019). Therefore, signaling power is exercised through this new type of gaze: an omniscient, centralized, dominating and vigilant gaze that guarantees transparency and visibility.

According to Foucault (1980) points out that Bentham raises the problem of visibility thinking of a visibility totally organized within the same dominating and vigilant gaze. That is why it is said that the idea that encouraged Bentham for the construction of a prison system was to solve the problem of surveillance. That is to say, that a single man would have a single power of surveillance that would overcome the forces gathered in large numbers.

Following Gutiérrez Zurdo's (2019) idea, Bentham's panopticon can be roughly defined as a place in which corresponds a form of complete surveillance implemented in a prison architecture and for penitentiary use.

1.1 Jeremy Bentham's architectural design of the panopticon

The panopticon model is described as follows: It has a circular layout on a central axis that locates a tower in which the watchman is located who has the ability to visually watch and supervise all the cells by hiding behind curtains. In reality, this structure allows the guard to stalk and watch over the entire area with the advantage that the inmates do not realize that they are being watched, creating a conscious state of absolute visibility, and that they can see without being perceived. In this way, a situation of power is established in which the observed himself is the one who provides that power.

Around the tower are located the prisoners' cells, individual, separated from each other and fully illuminated, without any point of shadow, because they have two windows: one open to the inside (of the tower) and the other to the outside so that light enters the cell. The aim is to ensure the good behavior of the inmates, and to increase security at the lowest possible cost, since fewer employees would be required to guard the prisoners.

Figure 1

Image of the architectural design of the panopticon.

Source: Pinterest.

The panopticon is based on control through observation. Individuals within the panopticon are completely exposed to the watchman's gaze. The watchtower is designed in such a way that the watchman can observe everything without being seen. Thus, the panopticon acts as a machine that separates the experiences of observing and being observed; outside the tower, one is fully visible without being able to see; in the central tower, one has a complete view without being perceived.

The main impact of this disciplinary model lies in inducing the prisoner into a constant state of visibility, which ensures the automatic operation of power. Even if the guard is not present or is observing another inmate, the prisoner cannot know, which means that he is unaware of when he is being observed and has no way of finding out. This asymmetry of information in the relationship between the watcher and prisoner is known as dissociation of the gaze, which Foucault (1980) introduces in 'The Eye of Power'. The objective of the panopticon is that the prisoner is forced to behave in a good way because he runs the risk of being punished for bad behavior, so he will tend to maintain a correct attitude and obedient to the imposed rules. Therefore, its effectiveness is not based on isolation or punishment, but on generating a conscious and permanent state of visibility that leads the subject to submit to the coercion of power by his own will.

As mentioned above, Foucault (1980) introduces three fundamental components for the functioning of the panopticon: awareness of surveillance, dissociation of the gaze and isolation.

The first component, surveillance awareness, refers to an individual who feels that he or she is constantly being watched by an unverifiable power. This leads to behaving in the right way under the influence of an authoritarian gaze. This form of domination reflects a clear superiority that manifests itself both in the subjects' perception and in their actions.

The dissociation of the gaze, as previously mentioned, establishes two clearly differentiated areas: the tower, from where one observes without being seen, and the cells, from where the individual is constantly observed without being able to know if he is being watched. Finally, the isolation to which the subjects are subjected is due to the reduction of unnecessary contacts. In other words, the individual is separated and classified individually so that the power of the gaze can exert its influence effectively, since it cannot be applied in the same way to an isolated individual as to a group.

1.2 Michel Foucault's reinterpretation of the panopticon: Surveillance and discipline.

Foucault takes the idea of the panopticon as a surveillance device implemented in all types of institutions (schools, factories, hospitals) in order to establish disciplinary systems. In his book, Watch and Punish, Foucault (2002) mentions that the panopticon functions as a generalizable model that defines the power relations in the daily life of man. In this way schools, hospitals, prisons and society govern and mold thought, constructing it under subjective norms implanted creating citizens who can be observed, conforming disciplinary societies.

The panoptic scheme is said to be ideal for imposing behaviors on a society, a way of making power relations work. Omniscient power and surveillance create in the individual self-control in the way he or she behaves; its efficacy is solidified in the action of seeing without being seen. For Foucault, the power of the panopticon creates automated and individualized subjects, who are observed. However, ignoring the watcher. The device erases singularities and imposes homogenization, it has the possibility of organizing, classifying, utilizing, recognizing its observers to guarantee control.

The panopticon is a machine that creates and sustains a relationship of power without relevance to the subject that exercises it. For Foucault (2002) the panopticon can be used as a machine to create experiences and modify the behavior of individuals, experiment with them, analyze transformations and obtain information.

The end of panopticism is the relations of discipline and is the general principle of the new political anatomy. Foucault situates disciplines from two extreme images; on the one hand, there is the discipline-blockade, which refers to closed institutions, with negative functions such as stopping evil or breaking communications, like quarantine. On the other hand, there is panopticism, the discipline-mechanism, a device that improves the functioning of power, making it faster, more agile, exercising coercion in a subtle way towards society. Thus, the formation of a disciplined society is giving rise to high productivity, centralization, acceptance of the norms and thoughts imposed by those in power.

The surveillance device is thus the relationship between power and discourse to produce subjectivities, truths, discourses and so on, to produce identities. It could be said that the device is the combination that makes up the elements and relationships that make control work, in short, it is the network. The production of subjectivities goes according to the convenience of those who exercise that power.

In the digital era, the panopticon is not limited to a physical structure of control, but manifests itself through platforms such as Facebook, Instagram, and X (Twitter), where users actively participate in a system of mutual surveillance. These social networks act as micro-panopticons, where each individual is not only observed, but also becomes an observer, thus contributing to a cycle of social control that feeds back on itself.

1.3 Evolution of control technologies since modernity.

The transition from the physical panopticon to a digital system began with the rise of information technologies during the 20th century. Tools such as surveillance cameras, centralized databases and the first computer networks became the pillars of a new control architecture; instead of direct supervision in closed spaces, these technologies introduced distributed, efficient and global surveillance.

Since the late 20th century, electronic performance monitoring (EPM) has been widely adopted in work environments to monitor employee performance. These technologies allow for systematic and continuous monitoring, facilitating the identification of training needs and improving productivity. OSHA (2022) states that employees have many recorded benefits from EPM such as helping to identify training needs, facilitating goal setting, translating productivity improvements, facilitating telecommuting and flextime, contributing to resource planning, among others.

Although these technologies monitor employee performance, they are not really concerned with employee welfare or privacy; OSHA (2022) states that a number of disadvantages have been associated with them, such as the following: they constitute a violation of the private sphere; increased stress levels and the possibility of worsening long-term health status; reduced levels of satisfaction and morale; reduced contact between workers and supervisors, as well as contact between co-workers, etc.

Fleischer in Altium (2024), states that Industrial Control Systems (ICS) are the backbone of modern industry, playing a crucial role in the operation and management of many processes. Through a combination of software and hardware, these systems monitor and regulate machinery, production lines and other activities. He also mentions that in today's rapidly evolving technological landscape, both the nature of industrial control systems and their integral components are constantly advancing and stresses the importance of electronic engineers staying informed about the latest trends, technologies and component innovations.

Supervisory Control and Data Acquisition Systems (SCADA) have evolved to manage complex industrial processes. These systems allow remote monitoring and control of critical infrastructures such as power grids and water treatment plants, integrating advanced technologies for efficient management. A variety of specialized formats exist to meet specific needs within the vast expanse of industrial operations. According to Altium (2024) one of the pillars of this domain is the Programmable Logic Controller (PLC). PLCs are rugged computers designed explicitly for industrial environments, playing an instrumental role in the control of a myriad of manufacturing processes.

Similarly, Altium (2024) mentions another critical type of system in the industrial control landscape is the Distributed Control System (DCS). Designed to serve processes within different areas or facilities. The capability of DCSs is powered by high-speed processors, redundant communication modules, and the integration of AI chips, which allow sophisticated analytical tasks to be performed. A having said this, it can be said that there are influential trends that shape the industrial control currently as they have had existence for over a century.

The incorporation of the Internet of Things (IoT) has revolutionized the industrial control landscape by enabling connected devices to collect and share data in real time. This improves operational efficiency and enables more detailed and personalized monitoring, reflecting an evolution towards more intelligent and adaptive systems. It also enables electronic engineers to implement intelligent, connected systems to collect real-time data and achieve monitoring and control capabilities.

Modern access control has also evolved from mechanical locks to advanced digital solutions that include biometric authentication and cloud-based platforms.

Technological evolution in control has had a profound impact on social and personal identity. Constant surveillance can lead to an internalization of social norms where individuals adjust their behavior according to what they believe is observed. This generates a dynamic where identity is influenced by the desire for conformity to the social expectations imposed by these technologies.

In addition, the increasing use of technologies that monitor personal aspects raises questions about privacy. Wearable devices that track health and well-being are clear examples of the potential to monitor not only work behaviors but also individual lifestyles.

The evolution of control technologies since modernity reflects a significant shift in how societies manage both individuals and organizational systems. From traditional panoptic models to today's AI- and loT-driven innovations, these technologies continue to shape our daily experiences and our identities in an increasingly interconnected and surveillance-driven world.

For their part, social networks represent a quantum leap in the evolution of the panopticon. Instead of being monitored exclusively by external institutions, users become active participants in their own surveillance. By sharing data, locations, interests and relationships, platforms create an 'inverted panopticon' where people voluntarily contribute to their monitoring.

Chapter 2: The digital panopticon

The digital panopticon is a term linked to the birth of the information society; that is, to the reflections on how new technologies make possible and facilitate the capture of user data. As for its main characteristics, we must point out that there is no longer the power of the watcher's gaze from a central perspective and without being seen, but the digital panopticon has a greater depth and capacity to capture information that is reflected in the multi-perspective work. All the subjects acquire the role of watchers and at the same time are watched; now the observation is produced from all angles, resulting in a crossed and unlimited surveillance. The illumination coming from all angles makes possible the elimination of blind spots: nothing goes unnoticed anymore, because it is a transparent system.

2.1 Definition of the digital panopticon

G arcía y García (2019) quotes Byung-Chul Han, in The Swarm (2016) who speaks of the panopticon, but now in a digital sense. In this sense it transcends Foucault's disciplinary society. About this new manifestation of the panopticon he notes that 'The digital society of surveillance displays a special panoptic structure. Bentham's panopticon consists of cells isolated from each other. Residents cannot communicate with each other. Walls make it impossible for the residents to see each other. In order to improve themselves, they are exposed to solitude. In contrast, the inhabitants of the digital panopticon create a network and communicate intensively with each other. What makes total control possible is not spatial and communicative isolation, but networking and hypercommunication.'

2.2 1984

Gutiérrez Zurdo (2019) relates a brief summary of George Orwell's novel 1984, he mentions that Orwell's story takes place in Oceania, one of the three world Superpowers where citizens follow a hierarchical pyramidal structure: at the top of this is Big Brother, in charge of watching endlessly through technological devices called tele-screens or from the multiple eyes of posters with this face observing and listening to all the spaces of the daily life of each subject (streets, workplaces, homes, etc.). At the same time, the figure of Big Brother is never represented in person, but it is the idea of a gaze; an all-encompassing gaze and therefore a gaze that prevents any intimacy.

Gutiérrez Zurdo (2019) says that the main plot of the book revolves around the life of Winston Smith and his attempts to rebel against the system. He is a worker of the Ministry of Truth whose function is based on rewriting or manipulating history to transform it according to the interests of the state. Similarly, there are three other ministries that watch over this great power: the Ministry of Love (in charge of administering punishments and martyrdoms), the Ministry of Peace (in charge of carrying out war-related matters by focusing on hatred and fear towards the outside world) and the Ministry of Abundance (in charge of economic tasks and rationing).

The story takes a turn when *Winston* meets *Julia* and they start a love relationship as, later on, together they will become a symbol of rebellion against system trying to fight against Big Brother. People like them, with rebellious instincts, secretly group together to form a society and have as their idol Goldstein, the main enemy of the Party. The protagonists, when discovered, are locked up by the Thought Police and subjected to numerous tortures in the Ministry of Love; where they end up accepting that the truth is what the Party says and not what they think or what they want. After coming out of their states of confinement, the couple is reunited, but they have no feelings of affection or love for each other. They have been defeated; the Party has managed to win that battle by replacing that love with love for Big Brother.

The book takes up the concept of the panopticon, as it reiterates the approach of a gaze as absolute power, as is Big Brother, who is omnipresent and whose control is exercised through telescreens and posters, since in this way he observes everything without being seen, and carries out repression. Since he is not represented as a concrete figure, it can be inferred that he is an invention or an abstraction used to dominate; similar to the watchman in the prison tower, since the prisoners were not aware whether there was anyone there or not.

However, in both scenarios, the notion of power expands from one subject to another, establishing itself deeply in each of them as a faithful, almost unwavering submission, which was generally motivated by the fear of being discovered by Big Brother who watches them in order to generate greater volume from the masses. Moreover, the efficacy of power is based on visibility, since the subject tends to self-submit, not knowing if he is being watched at that moment as it increases productivity and fosters a disciplinary society that seeks to correct individuals.

Today's society resembles a silent big brother, in charge of constantly monitoring through technological devices observing and listening to the spaces of the daily life of each subject (streets, workplaces, homes, etc.), which serves as a space of accumulation of an infinite number of aspects in which absolutely everything is recorded; from age, sex, residence, profession, user profiles, real-time location, leisure, interests, shopping, to the most personal tastes of each one. This information corresponds to what millions of people from all over the world have been depositing; so we are talking about an enormously high volume of figures. Therefore, as Fernández (2017) points out, the main characteristics of this method of data collection could be summarized as: volume, variety, veracity and speed.

2.3 Comparison between the classic and digital panopticon

A comparison between Bentham's classic panopticon and the contemporary digital panopticon reveals significant differences in the nature of surveillance and social control. In the original panopticon model, prisoners were aware that they could be observed at all times. This constant surveillance fostered internal discipline, as inmates adjusted their behavior in the knowledge that they were under the watchful eye of an invisible guardian. The structure of the panopticon created an environment of direct control, where the perception of being seen acted as a mechanism of authority.

In contrast, the digital panopticon operates in a context where people feel free as they actively share aspects of their personal lives on social media platforms. This phenomenon of digital exhibitionism manifests itself in the search for attention and social validation, where personal exposure becomes a means to gain recognition. However, this apparent freedom is deceptive. Unlike the classic panopticon, where surveillance was explicit, in the digital environment, control is subtle and omnipresent, as users voluntarily participate in their own surveillance by sharing personal information without due reflection.

Interaction with digital platforms fosters a process of self-surveillance, where individuals adjust their behavior and self-representation based on perceived social norms and expectations. As Ramonet (2016) points out, while Internet access can expand individual freedoms, it also provides governments and corporations with tools to conduct mass surveillance, intercepting communications and tracking online activities. This duality highlights how power is exercised in a camouflaged manner, where privacy becomes an increasingly scarce luxury.

Massive data collection and algorithmic analysis, characteristics of the digital panopticon, allow platforms to manipulate perceptions and behaviors in ways that users do not always fully understand. A collaborative phenomenon of surveillance is created in which each individual, by sharing data, contributes to the system that controls them. This raises serious ethical questions about autonomy and identity in the digital age, as users' ability to act freely is compromised by an environment that constantly observes and evaluates them. Digital surveillance, therefore, not only reflects a change in the methods of control, but also transforms the relationship between the individual and power in contemporary society.

Chapter 3: Digital surveillance

Digital surveillance refers to the practice of monitoring and collecting information about users' activities in digital environments. This surveillance can be carried out by various entities, including governments, corporations and non-profit organizations, using advanced technologies to track, analyze and store data. It often manifests itself through the collection of personal data, tracking of online behavior and monitoring of digital communication.

With the advent of the digital age, the ability to collect and process large volumes of data has grown exponentially. Tools such as cookies and analytics algorithms allow entities to observe user behavior in real time. According to Zuboff (2020), 'surveillance has become a new form of social control that captures the human experience for the surveillance economy'.

Many governments justify digital surveillance in the name of national security. Similarly, companies use surveillance to personalize the user experience, thereby enhancing their investment environment. In The Age of Surveillance Capitalism: The Struggle for a Human Future at the New Frontier of Power, Zuboff expands this definition by including the economic dimension. For her, digital surveillance operates not only in the sphere of state control, but also as a central tool in the economic model of technology companies. Zuboff (2020), 'Digital surveillance has become a new form of capital accumulation, where every digitizable action generates data that are exploited to predict and manipulate behaviors'.

For his part, Ramonet et. al (2016) states that in a way, surveillance has been 'privatized and democratized'. It is no longer exclusive to government intelligence services. Moreover, due to the close collaborations between states and large corporations leading the IT and telecommunications industries, the ability to conduct mass espionage has increased significantly.

In an interview with the WikiLeaks founder, he states that different companies such as Google, Apple, Microsoft, Amazon and recently Facebook, have established connections with the state apparatus in Washington, especially with foreign policy makers. Such a connection remains in evidence, as they share the same political ideas and have an equal vision of the world. Ultimately, the link and worldview with Google and the US administration serve US foreign policy objectives.

Such an unprecedented alliance of the state, the military security apparatus and the giant web industries has created a surveillance empire, the goal of which is straightforward. To bring the Internet under its command.

3.1 Definition of digital surveillance

Bartolomé (2021) says that digital surveillance refers to the observation of personal information intentionally, routinely and systematically for purposes of control, law and legitimacy, management, influence or protection. Although this activity is far from being new, its forms and methods have adapted to new technological possibilities, using Big Data and AI to identify and recognize patterns of behavior, automatically and massively.

Digital surveillance involves the detection, analysis and monitoring of information that can be potentially damaging. This includes identifying suspicious network activity, monitoring online reputation and protecting against cyber-attacks. Digital surveillance uses various technological tools, such as intrusion detection systems (IDS), behavioral analysis and social network monitoring, to provide a comprehensive view of an organization's security status.

The massive collection of personal data has transformed the notion of privacy into a luxury. Digital platforms, by capturing information on behaviors, preferences and interactions, create detailed profiles of users without their full consent. This situation not only infringes on the right to privacy, but also generates an almost omnipresent surveillance state where individuals are constantly observed and analyzed. As Zuboff (2020) points out, this lack of privacy can lead to a normalization of surveillance, where users unquestioningly accept the control exercised over them.

Digital surveillance also affects social norms by establishing a framework where certain behaviors are normalized and others are penalized. The pressure to conform to these norms can lead to a homogenization of thought and behavior, limiting individual diversity and creativity. The digital panopticon acts as a device that reinforces existing social hierarchies and perpetuates unequal power relations.

In modern society, where Information and Communication Technologies (ICT) are ubiquitous, digital surveillance intensifies users' perception of themselves and others. Social networks, for example, create a space where individuals become simultaneously observers and observed. The need to present an 'ideal' image to others can lead to constant comparison and personal evaluation, affecting self-esteem and mental health.

Digital surveillance also affects how individuals perceive others. The constant availability of personal information and the ability to observe others' interactions create an environment where social judgment becomes pervasive. Individuals can be evaluated not only by their actions, but also by their digital presence, creating a space of continuous competition and evaluation. This dynamic gives rise to stigmas and prejudices, as identities are shaped by superficial perceptions based on online interactions.

Digital surveillance, understood as the ability to observe and analyze online behaviors and interactions, has a significant impact on individual behavior. This phenomenon is not only limited to data collection by companies and governments, but also includes the self-surveillance that arises from the awareness of being watched.

Surveillance awareness transforms the way individuals behave online. Knowing that their actions are visible to others, users tend to self-censor and adjust their behavior to meet social expectations. This effect, known as 'living room behavior', refers to the modification of actions based on the perception of being watched. In this sense, digital surveillance acts as a control mechanism that promotes conformity and discourages disagreement.

In addition, massive data collection and algorithmic analysis allow platforms to manipulate the user experience, directing the content they view and the interactions they have. This can lead to a construction of information bubbles, where individuals are exposed primarily to opinions and perspectives that reinforce their pre-existing beliefs, limiting dialogue and diversity of thought.

Technological platforms, by exercising control over information and interactions, become power players that influence public opinion and decision-making. This power is exercised subtly but effectively, as users are often not fully aware of how their data is used to manipulate behaviors and perceptions. Digital surveillance has transformed power dynamics in several ways:

Decentralization of power: Unlike traditional power structures , where control is exercised by a specific entity, in the digital age power is dispersed. Each individual has the potential to be both watcher and watched, creating a more complex and subtle network of control.

Normalization of behaviors: Constant exposure to digital surveillance leads individuals to adopt behaviors that are perceived as socially acceptable. This translates into a normalization that perpetuates certain ideologies and practices.

Resistance and autonomy: Despite the pressure of surveillance, some individuals find ways to resist and disrupt these power dynamics. The use of privacy tools and the creation of alternative digital spaces are examples of how resistance can manifest itself in the age of surveillance.

3.2 Surveillance tools and technologies

According to Data 101 (n.d.), 'one of the main tools used in digital surveillance is the intrusion detection system (IDS). These systems analyze network traffic for anomalous patterns and behaviors that could indicate infiltration attempts. Upon identifying suspicious activity, IDSs trigger alerts so that security analysts can investigate and take appropriate action.'

Similarly, he mentions 'another key technology in digital surveillance is behavioral analysis. These systems use advanced algorithms and models to identify patterns of normal behavior in users and systems. By detecting significant deviations from these patterns, such as changes in access patterns or unusual activity, behavioral analytics systems can flag potential threats and help prevent attacks before they occur.'

Social media monitoring also enables organizations to track mentions and manage their online reputation by identifying fake profiles or harmful content, as well as continuously analyze large volumes of data to identify anomalies and suspicious patterns. This proactive approach helps to make informed decisions quickly and respond to potential threats before they cause harm.

Security Information and Event Management (SIEM) systems collect and analyze security data from various sources, providing a comprehensive view of the organization's security status. These systems are crucial to efficiently detect, respond to and manage security incidents.

One of the most widely used and advanced tools in digital surveillance is Artificial Intelligence (AI) and machine learning, which are revolutionizing digital surveillance by enabling advanced data analysis. These technologies can identify complex patterns and predict anomalous behavior, which significantly improves the ability to anticipate cyberattacks.

With the constant increase in cyber threats, advanced cybersecurity solutions are essential. This includes the use of firewalls, antivirus and vulnerability scanners, which help protect systems against unauthorized access and malicious attacks.

Automation and robotics, meanwhile, are beginning to play an important role in digital surveillance, especially in physical security. Robots equipped with advanced sensors can patrol large areas, while automated systems can manage access using technologies such as facial recognition on mobile and portable devices.

Active monitoring of social networks is vital to protect corporate reputation. Specialized tools are available to identify fake profiles, impersonations and harmful content that could affect an organization's public image.

The aforementioned tools and technologies are essential to establish a robust digital surveillance system that protects organizations against growing cyber threats. The effective implementation of these solutions not only improves security, but also enables a faster response to incidents, thus ensuring the integrity and availability of digital assets.

3.3 Control and self-monitoring mechanisms

The digital era has radically transformed the mechanisms of social control, introducing new dynamics that affect both governance and the daily lives of individuals. As technologies advance, sophisticated tools have been developed that enable unprecedented surveillance and control. These mechanisms are used not only by governments, but also by private companies, raising serious implications for privacy, autonomy and individual freedom.

One of the most notorious control mechanisms in the digital era is mass surveillance. This practice has intensified with the use of technologies such as internet-connected security cameras, drones and facial recognition software. Governments and corporations can collect large volumes of data on citizens' activities, allowing for constant monitoring. This type of surveillance raises concerns about invasion of privacy and potential abuse of power.

An example of this is in the People's Republic of China, the government has implemented a system of social control that uses advanced technologies to monitor its citizens, promoting a culture of conformity and obedience through fear of social and legal repercussions.

Consensual monitoring resembles how individuals, often without realizing it, agree to participate in their own surveillance when using digital platforms. By signing up for social networks or mobile apps, users provide personal data that are used to target advertising or influence behaviors. Following Rubio's (2020) idea, applications such as Facebook not only enable social interaction, but also act as control devices by collecting data on preferences and behaviors, using this information to manipulate the content presented.

Emerging technologies, such as loT and AI, have further expanded control capabilities. Devices even more control capabilities. Connected devices can collect data on daily habits, from energy consumption to health patterns, enabling detailed monitoring that can be used for both profit and social control. According to Carrasco Diaz-Masa (2021) states that the integration of loT into everyday life poses significant challenges to individual privacy. The constant collection of data can be used by governments or corporations to exert control over personal behaviors and decisions.

In the face of these challenges, it is essential to establish a clear regulatory framework that protects individual rights against the abusive use of control technologies. Digital literacy becomes essential to train citizens to identify disinformation and understand the workings behind digital platforms.

Today, platforms such as Facebook, Instagram and X (Twitter) act as micro-panopticons, where users are not only observed, but also become observers of others. This phenomenon creates a cycle of mutual surveillance that perpetuates social control. By sharing personal information and following the interactions of others, users actively contribute to their own and their peers' surveillance, which Foucault (2002) identified as a self-surveillance mechanism.

Self-monitoring refers to the practice in which individuals regulate their own behavior based on the social expectations and norms they perceive through their interactions on digital platforms. This concept is based on the idea that, being aware that their actions are visible to others, users adjust their behaviors to align with what they consider acceptable or desirable. Thus, surveillance becomes an internal process of self-regulation and results in conformity that limits personal authenticity. To which Ramonet et al (2016) argues that this normativity imposed by the digital environment generates pressure to present oneself in a way that obtains social validation, which can lead to a fragmentation of identity.

Likewise, Ramonet et al. (2016) mention that this phenomenon is particularly prevalent in social networks, where the search for validation through 'likes', comments and shares generates a constant pressure to present oneself in an attractive way and in accordance with the expectations of the environment. The need for social acceptance can lead individuals to modify their language, opinions and even their physical appearance, creating an idealized version of themselves that may not reflect their true identity. This process of personal curation, although it may seem harmless, induces a fragmentation of identity, where authenticity is sacrificed in favor of conformity.

Normativity in the context of self-policing refers to the way in which digital platforms establish and reinforce norms about how users should behave. These often invisible norms are shaped by the content that is promoted, the interactions that are celebrated and those that are sanctioned. Platforms use algorithms that not only determine what content is invisible, but also create an environment in which certain behaviors are normalized and others are discouraged.

For example, on Instagram, the image culture and the need to obtain 'likes' fosters a normativity that prioritizes appearance over authenticity. According to Zuboff (2020) this translates into a cycle where users feel pressured to follow trends, use filters and present an idealized life in order to be accepted. As a result, self-surveillance and normativity become intertwined, creating an environment where conformity is rewarded and deviation is penalized, although this penalization is not always explicitly manifested.

The implications of this self-surveillance are profound. The constant pressure to meet social expectations can lead to anxiety, depression and low self-esteem, especially among young people who are in the process of forming their identity. Constant comparison with others can lead to a distorted perception of reality, where experiences shared online appear to be more valuable than personal experiences.

In addition, the normativity imposed by digital platforms contributes to the homogenization of thought and behavior. By encouraging certain lifestyles and values, it limits the diversity of expressions and identities in the digital space. This can result in the creation of an environment where originality is discouraged and dissenting voices are silenced.

Self-surveillance and normativity are two sides of the same coin in the digital age. While self-policing empowers users to control their behavior, it can also lead to conformity and loss of authenticity. On the other hand, the normativity imposed by digital platforms creates a framework that defines what is acceptable and what is not, contributing to cultural homogenization. Together, these dynamics shape individual and collective identity, underscoring the need for critical reflection on the use of digital technologies and their effects on society.

3.4 Recommendation algorithms and their impact on individual autonomy.

Recommendation algorithms are fundamental tools in the digital age that allow to personalize the user experience by offering suggestions for content, products or services based on their preferences and past behaviors. These algorithms are used by platforms such as Netflix, Amazon, Spotify, Facebook, TikTok, Instagram and other social networks to improve user interaction and increase satisfaction, or to shape the information they consume and manipulate it. These systems identify patterns and predict future behaviors, feeding a feedback loop that influences consumption decisions, political preferences and social interactions as they play a crucial role in social control by determining what information is presented to users on digital platforms. These tools can personalize the content people see, creating echo chambers where they are only exposed to like-minded perspectives. This not only limits access to diverse information, but can also polarize opinions and foster social divisions. The manipulation of information through social media has led to the spread of disinformation and conspiracy theories, eroding trust in traditional media and hindering informed public dialogue. However, their use also raises questions about individual autonomy and control over personal decisions.

Recommendation algorithms are said to work primarily through two approaches, collaborative filtering that is based on the interactions and ratings of other users with similar tastes. For example, if a user A has similar preferences to a user B, the system will recommend to A that content that B has enjoyed. This approach can be explicit, through direct ratings in the applications themselves, or implicit, through behavioral analysis.

Content-based filtering, on the other hand, focuses on the characteristics of the items that the user has previously consumed, since it analyzes the attributes of the products or content (such as genre, author or topic) and suggests others that share similar content. Although many modern systems combine both approaches to improve the accuracy of recommendations, taking advantage of the benefits of each and mitigating their disadvantages.

Despite the benefits of recommendation algorithms, their use also has significant implications for individual autonomy. Constant comparison with the representations of others in social networks can distort individuals' perception of reality. By observing seemingly perfect lives, many may feel inadequate or dissatisfied with their own experiences, leading to a split identity and devaluing the authentic in favor of the superficial.

Individual autonomy is compromised in an environment where users believe they have control over their personal information by deciding what to share. However, this perception is misleading. These algorithms influence decisions and behaviors without users being fully aware of it.

While platform personalization can enhance the user experience by facilitating the discovery of relevant content, it can lead to 'polarization'. Users can become trapped in 'filter bubbles', where they are only presented with information that reinforces their existing beliefs, limiting their exposure to diverse perspectives. This can affect their critical capacity and willingness to explore new ideas.

Increasing reliance on these recommendations can lead to a decline in an individual's ability to make informed decisions on their own. By relying on algorithms to select content or products, users may lose critical skills to independently evaluate options. Platforms can use algorithms not only to personalize experiences, but also to manipulate behaviors.

For example, by prioritizing certain types of content over others, they can influence users' purchasing decisions or political opinions. This raises ethical questions about the control these platforms have over the information we consume.

Similarly, algorithms can perpetuate inequalities by favoring certain types of content that are more profitable or popular, affecting cultural diversity by limiting equal access to varied information.

Recommendation algorithms are powerful tools that have transformed the way we interact with digital content. However, their impact on individual autonomy is complex and multifaceted. While they offer convenience and personalization, they also present significant risks related to polarization, technological dependency and information manipulation. It is essential that both users and developers are aware of these effects to encourage a more conscious and critical use of these technologies.

3.5 Comparison between the digital panopticon and digital surveillance.

Conceptually, although both focus on the digital, it does not mean that they are exactly the same. On the contrary, while the panopticon refers to the structure of control and surveillance in which individuals are constantly observed through digital platforms. The digital panopticon implies that users are aware that they can be watched, which influences their behavior. Surveillance is based on the idea that the possibility of being observed generates self-control and compliance.

Digital surveillance, on the other hand, refers to the broader practice of monitoring and collecting data on users' activities in digital environments. This can include the collection of information by governments, corporations and other entities, often without users' knowledge or consent. Surveillance does not always involve individuals being aware that they are being watched, unlike the panopticon in which they are aware that they are simultaneously being watched.

Based on its control methods, the panopticon uses tools such as social networks, mobile applications and connected devices to encourage self-surveillance. Users, by sharing information about themselves, actively participate in their own surveillance. It is evident how individuals adjust their online behavior to be part of the social expectations and norms of the platforms. On the other hand, digital surveillance employs technologies such as data tracking, behavioral analysis and personal information collection. This type of surveillance can be carried out without the user being aware of it, and is often justified in the name of security or personalization of services.

That is, while the digital panopticon focuses on self-surveillance and social compliance in an environment where the possibility of being watched influences behavior, digital surveillance encompasses a broader range of monitoring practices that can occur without the user's knowledge.

Chapter 4: Social networks as surveillance spaces

Social networks have revolutionized the way we communicate and share information. However, behind their usefulness and convenience, there are hidden dynamics of surveillance that profoundly impact the lives of users, especially young people. These platforms function not only as spaces for social interaction, but also as environments where surveillance has become normalized, affecting the construction of identities and the privacy of individuals.

Social networks, such as Facebook, Instagram and TikTok, collect vast amounts of data about their users. Every "like," comment and post becomes part of a digital profile that companies use to create behavioral profiles. Not only does this allow the platforms to deliver personalized advertising, but it also translates into a form of constant surveillance. Users are monitored in real time, creating an environment where every action can be observed and analyzed.

The public nature of social networks creates an inherent pressure for users to present themselves in an attractive and successful way. This phenomenon, often referred to as "performativity," means that young people feel the need to curate their online image, displaying only the most positive aspects of their lives. This quest for social approval can lead to a distortion of identity, where users are more concerned with how they are perceived than with their authenticity.

For example, on platforms such as Instagram, it is common to see perfectly edited images and idealized life moments. This representation can make others feel inadequate or dissatisfied with their own lives, which reinforces anxiety and social pressure. The need to get "likes" and positive comments becomes a goal, often affecting users' mental health.

The panopticon is especially relevant in the context of social networks. In this surveillance model, individuals are observed without knowing when they are being watched, which influences their behavior. In the digital world, users often feel watched, which can lead them to modify their behavior to meet the expectations of others. This surveillance comes not only from platforms, but also from peers, who can judge and comment on what is posted.

As surveillance has become a normalized part of the social networking experience, users, especially young people, may come to accept this dynamic as second nature. This can lead to a lack of awareness of the implications of constant exposure. The idea that "if it's not online, it doesn't exist" reinforces the notion that life must be documented and shared, which perpetuates the cycle of surveillance.

A clear example of this is *Speed,* who during one of his live broadcasts, TikToker Speed experienced a terrifying moment when the police came to his house due to a "swatting" prank, which is when a person calls the officers for altercations or serious things happening.

Speed while he was distracted interacting with his followers, someone faked an emergency, leading armed agents to break into his home. This incident highlighted the dangers of attention-seeking on social networks, where users become alarmed at being watched and unaware of people's wrongdoing.

In addition, Speed's situation highlights how we are constantly under surveillance in the digital age. Continuous exposure on social platforms can lead to pranks turning into dangerous situations, showing that the fine line between spectacle and risk can have real and serious consequences. This case invites reflection on the responsibility we all have when interacting in a world where visibility can lead to unexpected and potentially harmful outcomes.

4.1 The construction of digital identities under constant surveillance

In the digital age, the construction of identities has been radically transformed, especially for young people who have grown up in an environment where technology and social networks are omnipresent. This new reality raises a significant issue: the constant surveillance young people face not only affects how they see themselves, but also how they choose to present themselves to the world. The pressure to be watched and evaluated in every digital interaction can lead to a distortion of identity, creating a space where authenticity is compromised.

As explained above, digital surveillance manifests itself in multiple ways. From data collection by platforms such as Facebook, Instagram and TikTok, to the social pressure to be "seen" and "accepted", young people are constantly aware that their actions are under the scrutiny of their peers. This phenomenon can be understood through the concept of the panopticon, as in the digital context, every post, comment and "like" becomes a public act that can be scrutinized and judged, which generates constant pressure to conform to certain expectations.

The need for social approval becomes a powerful driver in the construction of digital identities. Young people often feel that their personal value is linked to the number of "likes" and comments they receive. This search for validation can lead to the creation of an idealized image, where negative or vulnerable aspects of life are hidden.

On platforms such as Instagram, it is common for users to share only the happiest and most exciting moments, which can make others feel that their life does not compare. This phenomenon not only affects self-esteem, but can also foster a cycle of anxiety and depression, as young people get caught in a constant comparison to the seemingly perfect lives of others.

Constant vigilance also creates an internal conflict between authenticity and the projection of a desired identity. Young people may feel pressured to act a certain way to fit in or be accepted, which can lead to a disconnect with their true selves. They ask themselves, "Am I really me online, or just what others want me to be?" This struggle for authenticity can result in an identity crisis, where young people are forced to navigate between the need to be accepted and the desire to be genuine.

A clear example of this problem can be seen in the phenomenon of "influencers". Many young people aspire to become influencers, but often get caught up in the need to maintain a perfect image and a lifestyle that is not always real. This desire to be seen and followed can lead to the creation of content that does not reflect their true life, but an edited and carefully curated version. The pressure to be constantly "interesting" and "attractive" can result in significant emotional drain.

The digital panopticon is not only about observation, but also about how that observation affects behavior. Constant surveillance can lead young people to act in ways they deem socially acceptable, rather than simply being authentic. This can result in a disconnect between their online life and their true selves. On the other hand, some young people are beginning to realize this pressure and are looking for ways to be authentic despite the surveillance. They create spaces where they can express themselves without fear of judgment, such as closed social networking groups or private chat rooms.

4.2 Self-exposure in social networks

Self-exposure on digital platforms has become a ubiquitous phenomenon in the daily lives of millions of people, especially among young people. By sharing moments of their lives through photos, videos and posts, users create a personal narrative that can be viewed and commented on by a potentially global audience. However, this practice, while it may seem harmless or even beneficial, carries a number of psychological, social and ethical implications.

Self-exposure on social networks such as Instagram, TikTok and Facebook has become normalized in contemporary culture. The ability to share experiences and get instant feedback has led many to document every aspect of their lives, from everyday moments to significant milestones. This culture of self-exposure is fueled by the desire for connection and validation, where "likes" and positive comments become ways to measure social approval.

There are various motivations for self-exposure on digital platforms such as the search for validation as many users seek approval from their peers through "likes" and comments. This need for validation can be especially intense in adolescents, who are at a crucial stage of identity development.

Identity construction is an important factor in self-exposure, as it allows individuals to construct and project an identity that they want others to recognize. Often, this involves carefully curating the image that is presented, choosing only the most positive aspects of life.

Likewise, many young people seek social connection in the way that sharing experiences online can facilitate connection with friends and family, as well as with people who share similar interests. However, this connection can be superficial, depending on the context and depth of the interactions.

Many of the individuals on networks experience creativity and self-expression, as for some, digital platforms are a medium for creativity and self-expression. Posting art, music or writing about personal experiences can be a way to share unique talents and perspectives.

However, these motivations could have significant consequences such as social pressure and the need to be constantly "interesting" or "perfect". This can lead to overwhelming pressure. Users may feel that they must maintain an idealized image, which can lead to anxiety and frustration in trying to have an image that is alien to their reality or even wanting to fit in with social expectations, regardless of their socioeconomic cultural context.

Disconnection from reality takes its toll on users, as people focus on documenting their lives for social media, they can lose sight of enjoying the moments themselves. The obsession with self-exposure can distract from the actual experience of living due to obsessive content consumption, often users tend to spend more time on their mobile device than doing extracurricular activities or exploring new hobbies, creating a distortion in their reality that separates them from what is projected on networks to real life.

The impact on self-esteem is a numerous feature in the lives of young adolescents as they tend to constantly compare with the seemingly perfect lives of others and can negatively affect their self-esteem and self-perception, even feeling inadequate if their own lives do not align with online representations.

An essential factor is privacy and security, as self-exposure also poses risks in terms of privacy. Sharing personal information can make users vulnerable to exploitation, cyberbullying or unwanted surveillance as they often ignore the privacy terms and conditions of the various platforms and are unaware of what they are subject to by accepting the terms and conditions.

It is important to recognize that self-exposure has a dual nature. On the one hand, it can foster connection and creativity; on the other, it can result in anxiety, social pressure, and vulnerability.

4.3 The role of social networks in the normalization of surveillance

Social networks have transformed the way users interact with each other, share information and construct their own identities. However, they have also played a crucial role in normalizing surveillance, both at the personal and societal levels. This phenomenon not only affects individual privacy, but also redefines the dynamics of power and control in the digital age.

Self-exposure is a central feature of social networks. Users share aspects of their daily lives, from trivial moments to important events, in an environment where visibility is valued. This culture of exposure not only drives individuals to share more, but also fosters a form of social surveillance where peers constantly monitor and evaluate each other's actions. The phrase "if it's not online, it doesn't exist" reflects how this dynamic has permeated social interactions.

Unlike traditional forms of surveillance, where control is exercised by an external authority, social networks have fostered a type of surveillance in which users themselves actively participate. This phenomenon can be seen in the way individuals share personal information and allow others to access their data. The acceptance of terms and conditions, often without reading, is a clear example of how users give up their privacy in favor of connectivity. This voluntary participation has normalized surveillance, making users comfortable with the idea of being watched and evaluated.

Surveillance on social networks has also contributed to the normalization of practices such as cyberbullying. The ease of access to personal information and the ability to monitor the actions of others have made some users feel empowered to harass or judge others. This environment of social surveillance can lead to devastating and even legal consequences.

The normalization of surveillance on social networks raises concerns about privacy and identity. As users share more of their lives online, there is an erosion of personal privacy. This not only affects how individuals perceive themselves, but also impacts their emotional well-being. The pressure to maintain a perfect public image can lead to the creation of distorted identities, where authenticity is sacrificed in favor of social approval.

4.4 The culture of digital stalking

Panoptic surveillance in the digital age and the culture of digital 'stalking' among youth are interconnected in ways that reveal the complexity of our relationship with technology and privacy. While governments use tools to monitor citizens, many young people seem to enjoy the attention they receive online, often sharing intimate aspects of their lives.

Marwick (2013) examines how the culture of self-exposure on social networks can lead to situations of digital stalking, arguing that the search for validation through "likes" and comments can make people more vulnerable to online harassment.

In recent decades, technological advances have allowed governments to implement more sophisticated surveillance systems. The use of the Internet and social networks has facilitated the collection of data on citizens. Platforms such as Facebook and Twitter have become tools not only for communication, but also for monitoring. Every "like", every tweet and every post become pieces of a puzzle that the state can use to understand and control the population.

An example of this could be a teenager who, after posting a photo, spends hours refreshing the screen, waiting for the "likes" to flow in. Each notification is a shot of adrenaline, but also a source of stress. How many "likes" are enough to feel accepted? This relentless search for approval creates a vicious cycle of anxiety and unease, where young people feel that their worth depends on their online presence.

Surveillance is no longer just a matter of control by external entities; it has infiltrated the daily lives of young people. The idea of being watched has become so commonplace that many do not question it. "Social surveillance" manifests itself in the way friends and followers analyze, criticize and comment on every post. This dynamic transforms interactions into a spectacle, where every action is evaluated not only for its content, but for its ability to attract attention.

Constant exposure and social surveillance can lead to the creation of fragmented identities, where young people feel the need to project idealized versions of themselves. Instead of being authentic, they become actors on a digital stage, playing roles that may not reflect who they really are. This dissonance between the real self and the digital self can generate an identity crisis, where the search for authenticity is undermined by the need to fit into a predefined social mold.

4.5 State surveillance

State surveillance has become a reality in many countries, with governments using advanced technologies to monitor citizens. This includes collecting data through social networks and implementing facial recognition systems. While this type of surveillance seeks to control and repress, it also creates an environment where young people are aware that their actions are being watched. However, many of them, instead of seeing this as a threat, adopt an attitude of exposure.

In this context of surveillance, young people often seek social validation through their online presence. The attention they receive on social networks reinforces their sense of identity and belonging. Each "like" or comment becomes an indicator of popularity, which can lead to increased exposure. This desire for recognition can be seen as a response to surveillance, as young people actively choose to show parts of their lives rather than hide them.

The need to construct an identity in an environment where surveillance is omnipresent can lead young people to share more than they normally would. Digital platforms become spaces where they can experiment and project an idealized image of themselves, often without considering the implications of this exposure. In this sense, digital "stalking" becomes a form of self-affirmation, where being observed is synonymous with being relevant.

Chapter 5: Psychological implications of digital surveillance.

The omnipresence of digital surveillance in everyday life through social networks, mobile devices and online platforms has profound psychological implications that affect the mental health and well-being of individuals. As technology advances, it is critical to understand how this form of constant observation impacts the human psyche, especially among young people, who are the most affected by these dynamics, as digital surveillance creates an environment of constant pressure.

Users, especially young users, may experience anxiety related to the need to present themselves perfectly on their online profiles. Worrying about how they will be perceived by others can lead to a state of permanent alertness, where every post becomes a source of stress. This anxiety can manifest itself in physical and emotional symptoms, including insomnia, irritability and concentration problems.

The search for validation through "likes" and comments on social networks can distort young people's perception of themselves. Their self-esteem becomes a numbers game, where personal worth is measured based on online interaction. This dependence on external approval can lead to feelings of inadequacy and devaluation, especially when expectations are not met.

The pressure to maintain a "perfect" identity online can result in a fragmentation of identity. Young people may feel the need to present different versions of themselves, adapting to the expectations of their audience. This can generate a disconnect between the real self and the digital self, which in turn leads to confusion and identity crisis. The struggle to be authentic in an environment that values image over reality can be overwhelming.

Digital surveillance has contributed to the normalization of cyberbullying, where negative comments and judgment become commonplace. This constant exposure to criticism can desensitize young people, making them more likely to engage in hurtful behavior. The experience of cyberbullying can have devastating effects on mental health, leading to depression, isolation and, in extreme cases, suicidal thoughts.

Miley Cyrus, famous for her role in Hannah Montana, is a clear example of how media surveillance can shape a celebrity's identity. From a young age, she lived under constant media scrutiny, trapped in the image of a 'Disney girl', which led her to a deep identity crisis. This pressure to be perfect and accepted pushed her to adopt a rebellious style, exemplified in her album ***Bangerz,*** sparking criticism and debates about her authenticity. The constant surveillance affected her mental health, leading her to experience anxiety and depression. However, Miley transformed her pain into power, using her platform to advocate for self-acceptance and freedom of expression. Her story highlights how digital surveillance not only impacts public perception, but can also distort personal reality, creating a disconnect between authentic self and projected image....

Constant surveillance can foster a sense of paranoia and distrust. Users may begin to question the intentions of those around them, fearing they will be watched or judged at any moment. This distrust can affect interpersonal relationships, creating an environment where open and honest communication is compromised.

Overexposure to digital surveillance can lead to privacy fatigue, where individuals feel exhausted by the need to manage their online image. This exhaustion can result in an apathy towards privacy, where young people stop caring about the implications of sharing their personal information. However, this lack of attention can have serious consequences, including personal data exploitation and cyberbullying.

The story of Britney Spears is a clear example of how constant surveillance can affect a public figure's mental health and identity. Since her meteoric rise in the music industry in the late 1990s, Spears was subjected to relentless scrutiny from the media and the public. The pressure to be 'the perfect pop girl' was intensified by the omnipresence of social media and gossip culture, where every move was analyzed and criticized.

This hostile environment reached its peak in 2007, when, after a series of traumatic events, such as her divorce from her husband and the loss of custody of her children, Britney suffered an emotional breakdown, which included self-destructive behaviors such as the famous incident in which she shaved her head. The surveillance not only contributed to her breakdown, but also led to her subsequent guardianship, which severely limited her autonomy for more than a decade. Britney's battle to regain control of her life resonates with many young people who struggle with societal expectations and the pressure of being constantly watched. Her story is a powerful reminder that behind every public image is a human being who can be deeply affected by societal surveillance and judgment.

5.1 Effects of surveillance on individual behavior

In the digital age, surveillance has become a constant in everyday life. From supervision in the workplace to monitoring on social networks, the feeling of being watched has penetrated every aspect of our existence. This phenomenon not only transforms the way we behave, but also alters interpersonal dynamics. In particular, surveillance profoundly affects performance and productivity in work environments, as well as trust in personal relationships. As we explore these issues, it becomes clear that surveillance, rather than being a tool for improvement, can become a trap that limits creativity and erodes trust.

In the workplace, monitoring presents itself as a double-edged sword. On the one hand, supervision can incentivize employees to maintain a high level of productivity. The idea of being watched often drives individuals to work harder, meet deadlines and achieve goals. However, this pressure can come at a high cost. When employees feel they are under a constant microscope, creativity and innovation can be stifled. The need to meet rigid standards can cause workers to adhere to predictable routines, fearful of deviating from what is expected of them.

Surveillance not only affects productivity; it also has a devastating impact on trust. When people feel watched, they tend to be more reserved and cautious in their interactions. This distrust can flourish in an environment where privacy is an illusion, creating an atmosphere of suspicion and suspicion. Interpersonal relationships, which should be a haven of support and understanding, become battlegrounds, where every word and action is evaluated under the lens of surveillance.

This dynamic is further complicated in the context of social networks, where constant exposure can make people feel insecure about how they are perceived by others.

In this space, surveillance is not only external; individuals also become their own watchdogs, carefully monitoring how they present themselves to their audience. This self-surveillance can lead to a lack of authenticity, where people feel the need to project idealized versions of themselves, fearful that any mistakes could be caught and used against them.

The result is a vicious cycle of distrust, where the need to maintain a perfect public image undermines sincerity in relationships. Conversations become superficial, bonds weaken and intimacy becomes an increasingly elusive concept. In a world where every interaction can be monitored and judged, authenticity is sacrificed on the altar of social approval.

5.2 FOMO effect

'Fear of Missing Out' (FOMO), or 'fear of missing out', is a term that describes the anxiety people feel when they believe they are missing out on rewarding experiences that others are enjoying. This phenomenon has become especially prevalent in the age of social networking, where people are constantly exposed to the activities and experiences of their friends and acquaintances.

This is intensified in a surveillance environment, as young people feel the pressure to always be connected and aware of what their peers are doing. This impulse can lead to overexposure on social networks, where moments of daily life are shared in an attempt not to be left out of the conversation. This phenomenon reflects how state surveillance and the desire for attention intertwine, creating a cycle in which self-expression is influenced by the need to be seen.

However, this culture of surveillance and exposure also has its risks. The pressure to be constantly visible can lead to mental health issues, such as anxiety and depression, especially if online validation does not translate into meaningful connections in real life. In addition, the lack of boundaries in self-presentation can result in negative repercussions, where the line between personal and public is blurred.

It is critical that young people begin to reevaluate their relationship to privacy in a world where state surveillance is a reality. Education about digital identity management and the importance of setting boundaries can be key. Learning to balance the need for self-expression with privacy protection can empower young people to navigate an environment where surveillance and exposure are part of everyday life.

In the digital age, panoptic surveillance has found a new field of application in the world of video games, where young people interact in increasingly connected virtual environments. Through data collection and online behavior monitoring, gamers become subjects of constant surveillance that they often do not fully recognize or understand. This lack of awareness can lead to a normalization of surveillance, where young people, driven by a desire for belonging and social validation, ignore the implications of being watched.

The Attention Economy: The Desperate Search for Likes and Its Cost.

The attention economy refers to how technology companies and content creators fight for users' time and attention. Every time we swipe through our feed or watch a viral video, we are participating in this competition. Algorithms are designed to keep us hooked, which means the content we consume is carefully curated to capture our attention.

In the digital age, attention has become the new gold. Platforms like TikTok have created an environment where the quest for likes and followers can lead content creators to do extreme things, often putting their safety and dignity at risk. This obsession with being seen and recognized can have devastating consequences.

Viral challenges on social networks are a clear example of this trend. Many young people feel pressured to participate in challenges that may be dangerous or humiliating just for the possibility of going viral. There have been documented cases of serious injuries and even accidental deaths due to challenges that began as simple trends on TikTok. The quest for attention can lead some to ignore the risks, driven by the promise of instant fame.

In addition to the physical risks, many creators sacrifice their pride and dignity in the pursuit of social validation.

A notable example is that of La Joela, a TikToker who, after losing a live challenge, decided to go naked in his transmission. This act, which could have been a form of humor or an impulsive reaction, quickly became an object of mockery and scorn on the platform. The public's reaction was relentless, and 'la Joela' became a meme, showing how the search for attention can turn into a humiliating experience.

These types of situations highlight a disturbing reality: for many, likes and comments have become a measure of personal value. Instead of building an identity based on who they really are, some young people are forced to play roles that go against their dignity, just to get that ephemeral validation offered by social networks.

Some examples are given of young people who seek fame through extreme challenges and have lost their lives and dignity.

Clear examples of these are as follows:

On July 30, 2019, a Chinese youtuber known as Sun, who was 35 years old, died a shocking death while broadcasting a live challenge via DouYou, China's YouTube equivalent platform. Sun was famous for his extreme videos and for constantly looking for ways to capture the attention of his audience, which led him to perform increasingly dangerous challenges. On this occasion, he decided to do a challenge that consisted of spinning a wheel with different food options and consuming whatever he got. However, what he chose was quite risky: he started eating poisonous centipedes and live salamanders, accompanied by vinegar and a local liquor called baijiu. As the video progressed, his behavior seemed increasingly bizarre; viewers noticed that he looked uncomfortable and struggled to stay conscious. As his 15,000 followers were glued to their screens, Sun suddenly faded away, falling to the ground without being able to react. The broadcast continued to air, revealing the tragic moment when his girlfriend found him lifeless shortly after. Police arrived on the scene and discovered that the camera was still recording, leaving all viewers in shock. DouYou, following the incident, decided to remove all videos from Sun's channel.

This tragic event underscores the dangers of viral challenges that have become popular on social media. Many young people seek quick fame and validation from their followers, often without considering the consequences of their actions. The quest for "likes" and views can lead to extreme situations and, as in Sun's case, to fatal endings.

Sun's story has sparked a debate about the responsibility of digital platforms and content creators in promoting dangerous behavior. As viral challenges continue to proliferate on the internet, it is vital that both creators and viewers reflect on the limits of fun and what they are really willing to risk for fame.

These types of situations highlight a disturbing reality: the quest for recognition on social networks can lead to extreme and dangerous decisions. The trend of taking pictures of oneself in risky places not only shows a lack of awareness of physical dangers, but also reveals a culture that values appearance over safety. Young people often feel pressured to do things that go against their common sense just to get a couple of extra likes or a few admiring comments. This raises an important question: how far are they willing to go for a moment of online fame?

The impact of this trend extends beyond individuals. The glorification of these actions on social networks creates a cycle in which people continue to repeat risky behaviors in an attempt to outdo others. Each new "challenge" or "trend" can become more extreme than the last, pushing young people into more dangerous situations. The need to be seen and validated in a digital world can lead to a disconnect with reality, causing many to underestimate the risk they are taking.

In this context, it is crucial to reflect on how we are constantly under surveillance in the digital age. The pressure to be seen and recognized can cause people to act in ways that compromise their safety. The quest for likes can cloud judgment, and what starts out as simple fun can turn into a traumatic experience. This phenomenon not only affects those seeking fame, but also has repercussions for those around them, from friends and family to the community at large.

Another case in point was The story of Wu Yongning, known as the "Chinese Spiderman," tragically illustrates the dangers of the trend known as rooftopping, which involves climbing tall buildings without safety equipment. Wu amassed thousands of followers on Weibo thanks to his daredevil stunts and his pursuit of extreme challenges to earn money and recognition. This pressure to maintain an exciting image led him to perform a dangerous live stunt, which culminated in his death when he fell from a 62-story building. His tragedy highlights how social surveillance-where viewers not only watch, but also encourage risky behavior-can influence the decisions of content creators. As rooftopping culture continues to grow, it is critical to reflect on the responsibility of platforms and creators, as well as the need to prioritize safety over virality, to prevent stories like Wu's from repeating themselves.

In short, the trend of taking pictures of oneself on the tops of buildings is a clear reflection of the culture of self-exposure and the economy of attention. As young people seek validation in a world where likes are currency, it is essential to remember that behind every image is a human being who deserves care and respect. The pressure to stand out can lead to dangerous choices, and it is vital to foster a culture that prioritizes safety and authenticity over superficial recognition.

The attention economy feeds a culture of dissatisfaction, where the constant search for approval can lead to a feeling of emptiness. Every like received is a small relief, but it is never enough. This cycle can lead to anxiety, depression and a constant need to be in the spotlight, leading to increasingly extreme and often self-destructive behaviors.

Chapter 6: Ethical and Social Implications of Surveillance

Surveillance in the digital age has transformed the way in which personal data are collected, analyzed and used. This chapter is structured in four sections that address the ethical and social implications through this practice, focusing on privacy, the role of Biga Data in the collection of personal information, and the ethical and legal dilemmas that arise in this context.

6.1 The ethics of surveillance

Surveillance ethics focuses on the moral principles that should guide the collection and use of personal data. As technologies advance, it becomes essential to evaluate the balance between the benefits of surveillance (such as surveillance and public health) and individual rights to privacy.

Surveillance ethics refers to the moral principles that govern the practice of observing and collecting information on individuals and groups. In this context, it is essential to question who has the right to conduct surveillance, for what purpose and under what conditions. According to Lyon (2016), surveillance should be evaluated, not only for its effectiveness but also for its impact on human dignity and individual rights. The ethics of surveillance involves a balance between public safety and privacy protection, where transparency and accountability are crucial to establish trust in the institutions that implement surveillance practices.

According to Perplexity AI (2024) Some of the key ethical principles are:

Transparency: Organizations should be clear about what data they collect, for what purpose, and how it will be used. Lack of transparency can erode public trust, as WHO (2024) argues that 'in the absence of trust, [individuals[will not report personal information or, if they do, it will be unreliable. If surveillance (in this case, of public health) addresses problematic ethical issues in advance and proactively seeks to reduce unnecessary risks, much will have been done to gain and maintain the trust of affected populations'.

It also mentions that 'Public health surveillance organizations or agencies must take into account the values, concerns, and priorities of the population in a transparent manner. Communities cannot be involved if they have no way of knowing the benefits and risks (or potential negative effects) of surveillance.'

Consent: It is essential to obtain informed consent from individuals before collecting their data. This implies that individuals should be fully aware of how their information will be used. In this regard, WHO (2024) notes that 'The main reference values of research ethics are autonomy, privacy and confidentiality. ' and 'Sometimes, data recorded during surveillance, such as names and addresses, allow individuals to be identified. The use of unique identifiers (e.g., numbers instead of names) is one way to avoid inadvertent disclosure of individuals' identities. Another method is "geographic masking," which serves to preserve a record of essential data on the distribution of cases but does not make it possible to know the exact location of clusters of cases. Assessing the legal instruments that protect those most likely to suffer harm is another strategy for ensuring that comprehensive social protection arrangements are in place prior to surveillance.'

Proportionality: Data collection should be proportional to the objective to be achieved. No more data should be collected than is necessary to fulfill a specific purpose.

6.2 Ethical implications of ubiquitous surveillance

Before starting with the ethical implications of ubiquitous surveillance, it is necessary to understand the concept of ubiquitous surveillance.

Ubiquitous surveillance refers to the ability to observe and collect data anytime, anywhere, thanks to technologies such as smartphones, security cameras and Internet of Things (IoT) devices. This form of surveillance raises serious ethical implications. Foucault (2002) mentions that the constant presence of monitoring devices can create an environment of anxiety and self-censorship, where individuals feel compelled to modify their behavior for fear of being watched. Furthermore, Zuboff (2019) argues that ubiquitous surveillance can erode privacy, a fundamental right, leading to a normalization of exposure and lack of safe spaces for privacy. This surveillance raises ethical concerns and an impact on privacy.

Constant monitoring can lead to a significant erosion of personal privacy. Individuals may feel that they have no control over their information, which can result in a state of anxiety and distrust of institutions.

Widespread acceptance of surveillance can lead to a normalization of monitoring in various spheres of life, from work to home. This may change social norms about what is considered acceptable in terms of privacy as mentioned by PAHO (2017), 'There are many different types of harm: economic, legal, psychological, social (as well as reputational), and physical. All of these should be considered in relation to surveillance (70-72). For example, through surveillance, a migrant or a person from another disadvantaged group could be identified as an individual at increased risk of an infectious disease, which could lead to stigmatization of the group. Relevant information must be handled very carefully: reputation can be damaged quickly, and the results can be devastating across a spectrum that may include types of harm not yet documented (73). Various moral values and ethical principles must be weighed and balanced against each other, and a conclusion must be reached as to the fair distribution of burdens and benefits in different surveillance initiatives or systems in a transparent manner.'

6.3 Big data and the massive collection of personal information

The rise of Big Data has enabled organizations to collect and analyze large volumes of personal information. While this can offer significant benefits, such as improvements in public services and personalized healthcare, it also raises serious ethical concerns.

Big Data' refers to the collection and analysis of large volumes of data, often in real time. While this practice can offer significant benefits, such as improving services and identifying patterns, it also raises serious ethical concerns. Fernandez (2017) says that, ' Big data as a trend arises, then, when industry realizes that it cannot store and manage information in a conventional way; it is therefore a logical step in the process of using ICT.'

Regan (1995) mentions that the massive collection of personal information is often done without the informed consent of individuals, which raises questions about autonomy and control over one's own data. Likewise, Cohen (2012) says that the use of algorithms to process these data can perpetuate existing biases and discriminate against certain groups, highlighting the need for stricter regulation and more ethical practices in data management.

Some risks associated with Big Data are:

Algorithmic discrimination: Algorithms can perpetuate existing biases if fed with biased data, which can result in unfair decisions in areas such as employment, credit or health care.

Lack of Control: Individuals often lack control over their data once it is collected. This can lead to situations where their information is used without their knowledge or consent.

Data Security: Bulk collection increases the risk of security breaches, exposing sensitive information to cyber attacks.

6.4 Ethical and legal dilemmas in the digital age

The digital age presents a number of ethical and legal dilemmas related to surveillance. As technologies evolve faster than the laws that regulate them, significant challenges arise. Cohen (2012) notes that one of these is the lack of adequate legislation to protect the privacy of individuals in an environment where data are collected so extensively. Regulations, such as the General Data Protection Regulation (GDPR) in Europe, have begun to address these issues, but there is still a long way to go. In addition, the rapid evolution of technology often outpaces the ability of laws to adapt, creating a regulatory vacuum. This context raises questions about the responsibility of companies and governments in protecting citizens' rights, as well as the need for a legal framework that ensures transparency and fairness in surveillance practices.

Some of the legal challenges are inadequate regulation, as although there are many existing laws, they are not equipped to address the complex issues associated with digital surveillance, creating a legal vacuum that can be exploited by organizations. On the other hand, there are confusing jurisdictions, as the global nature of the Internet further complicates legal compliance, as different countries have different standards on privacy and data protection.

Among the ethical considerations is the corporate responsibility of companies, as they must take responsibility for how they use personal data. This includes implementing ethical practices in the handling of sensitive information. Also, surveillance must not compromise fundamental human rights, as it is essential to ensure that surveillance practices respect these rights and do not lead to abuses.

In other words, the ethical and social implications of the digital era are complex and multifaceted, requiring careful and critical consideration. It is essential to establish a sound ethical framework to guide personal data collection and use practices, thus ensuring a balance between public safety and respect for individual rights. It is essential that society addresses these challenges by promoting awareness of them, for surveillance should be a tool for security and well-being, not a means for control and oppression.

Chapter 7: Resistance to the digital panopticon

The internalization of this social control generates a profound impact on individual behavior, leading to conformity, anxiety and distrust in interpersonal relationships. However, as surveillance becomes the norm, significant resistance also emerges. Through privacy awareness, the use of data protection technologies, and collective activism, individuals find ways to oppose surveillance and reclaim their autonomy.

One of the most effective forms of resistance to the digital panopticon is awareness of surveillance practices and digital privacy education. As more people become informed about how their data is collected, used and shared, they begin to question the normalization of surveillance. This awareness can lead to changes in behavior, such as using stricter privacy settings on social networks, choosing platforms that prioritize data security, and using encryption tools. Digital education empowers users to make informed decisions about their online presence, thus challenging the control exercised by corporations and governments.

Resistance to the digital panopticon also manifests itself in the use of technologies designed to protect privacy. Tools such as privacy-focused browsers (such as Tor), encrypted messaging applications (such as Signal) and browser extensions that block trackers (such as uBlock Origin) are examples of how individuals can protect themselves from surveillance. These technologies allow users to navigate the digital world with a greater sense of security, hindering the surveillance capabilities of external actors. The use of VPNs (virtual private networks) has also become popular as a way to hide online activity and evade monitoring.

Some of these applications are Signal, NordVPN or ExpressVPN, Brave or Firefox Focus, DuckDuckGo, Jumbo privacy, etc. These applications help to manage privacy on social networks and other online services, block ads and trackers by default or serve to remove traces of personal information.

Some Instagram users have promoted the use of tracker blocking tools and private browsers to protect their personal information. In addition, they have shared information on how to enable privacy options on their accounts, such as turning off location tracking or limiting who can see their stories.

Resistance to the digital panopticon is not limited to individual actions; it also manifests itself in collective movements and activism. Groups such as the Electronic Frontier Foundation (EFF) and Privacy International work to advocate for policies that protect privacy and freedom in the digital environment. These organizations raise public awareness of the implications of surveillance and fight against legislation that threatens privacy. In addition, online protests and campaigns have emerged to challenge state and corporate surveillance, raising awareness of the importance of privacy as a human right.

Now it is noticeable that on TikTok, content creators have started making "informational videos" that explain how to protect online privacy. For example, , some users post tutorials on how to adjust privacy settings in the app, helping others to be more aware of how their data is used.

Resistance is also expressed through digital subcultures that challenge established norms. From the use of memes and humor to criticize surveillance to decentralized platforms that promote privacy, these forms of digital counterculture create a space for dissent.

On YouTube, a movement has emerged around demonetization and censorship of content that addresses surveillance and privacy issues. Creators such as "ContraPoints" and "Philosophy Tube" have used their platforms to criticize large corporations' policies around privacy, promoting the idea that users should have more control over their data.

DeleteFacebook, this arose in response to concerns about privacy and data misuse by the platform. Many people decided to delete their Facebook accounts as a form of collective protest against surveillance and control of personal data.

Resistance to the digital panopticon implies a rejection of the normalization of surveillance. As surveillance becomes an accepted part of everyday life, people begin to question this acceptance. Resistance can manifest itself in a refusal to participate in platforms that sacrifice privacy for convenience, as well as a critique of the "share-it-all" culture. This rejection of standardization invites a deeper reflection on the cost of surveillance on individual freedom and autonomy.

On TikTok, there is a trend of videos critiquing the culture of "perfect content." Users are promoting authenticity and vulnerability, sharing personal and imperfect experiences to challenge the pressure to conform to standards of beauty or success imposed by the platform. This translates into a rejection of social surveillance and the need to project an idcalized image.

These examples on platforms such as TikTok, YouTube and Instagram illustrate how users are taking action to resist digital surveillance. Through education, promotion of authenticity, collective activism and rejection of the normalization of surveillance, individuals are challenging the dynamics of control and reclaiming their right to privacy in an increasingly surveilled environment.

7.1 State surveillance and social control.

Imagine that every time you share something on social networks, there is an invisible 'eye' watching you. That is the essence of state surveillance as governments and institutions use technology to monitor what individuals do, say and, in some cases, even what they think. Although it may sound like a science fiction movie, it is more real than you think.

It works in different ways, as there are surveillance and social control technologies, starting with cameras everywhere, from streets to stores, cameras are everywhere. These not only record, but often use artificial intelligence to analyze behaviors and detect 'suspicious activity'. Just like every time you use an app or browse the internet, a data trail is left behind. This "big data" can be used to profile each subject, which means they know who each person is and what they like, even before they know it.

It is important because it has a significant impact on freedom; state surveillance can threaten people's freedom of expression. For, at times, they may come to feel that their words and actions are being monitored, so they would choose not to share their thoughts or not to show themselves in general, generating an impoverishment of dialogue and limiting the diversity of ideas.

When individuals feel threatened, they consider surveillance to become the norm, creating an environment in which everyone feels insecure and distrustful, thus leading people to avoid discussing issues of importance, such as politics or social justice, for fear of repercussion; creating a culture of fear.

7.2 The role of personal data legislation.

Imagine that every time you use your phone or surf the Internet, you leave a digital footprint. Those footprints are your data: photos, messages, searches, likes and dislikes and more. Now, what if I told you that these footprints are often collected by companies and governments without you even realizing it? This is where personal data legislation comes in, a set of rules that protects your privacy in the vast digital ocean.

Today, we live in a hyper-connected world. From social networks to streaming applications, personal information is constantly being shared. The goal of personal data legislation is to ensure that personal data is treated with respect and that individuals have control over it.

One of the key principles of data legislation is "informed consent". This means that companies must ask individuals for permission before using their personal data. Not only that, but there must be a clear and simple explanation of how it will be used.

Personal data legislation grants the "right to know". This means that every individual has the right to ask companies what data they hold about them and how they are using it. This right not only empowers individuals; it also encourages transparency. Companies know they can be questioned, which motivates them to be more careful with the information they handle.

Sometimes, personal data may be incorrect, which is why the legislation grants the "right to correct" such data. If inaccurate information is found, you can request that it be corrected. This is especially important in situations such as job searches, where a simple inaccuracy can affect a person's future.

Maintaining data accuracy is crucial. In a world where decisions are increasingly made based on algorithms, making sure that each person's personal information is correct is vital to protect your opportunities and reputation.

Similarly, personal data legislation also establishes rules on how companies must protect such information. This includes implementing security measures to prevent hackers from accessing data. Thinking of it as a digital shield, companies are obliged to invest in security to protect the information of many; reducing the risk of data breaches that could jeopardize the privacy of individuals.

Laws not only protect users; they also hold companies accountable. If a company does not comply with regulations, it can face severe penalties. This creates an incentive for companies to handle data ethically. This approach promotes a change in corporate culture.

As technology advances, personal data legislation becomes even more relevant. With the advent of new technologies, such as artificial intelligence and big data, it is crucial that laws adapt to address emerging challenges. It is vitally important that young people are informed about their rights and how they can protect their information. Knowing the law empowers you to navigate the digital world with confidence and security.

7.3 Future of digital surveillance.

You're in a coffee shop with your friends, enjoying a coffee and sharing memes. It all seems normal, right? But here's the thing: while you're laughing, your smartphone is collecting data about you: what you like, who you hang out with, even your emotions at that moment. Technology is advancing by leaps and bounds, and digital surveillance is becoming part of our daily lives, almost without us even realizing it. But what does this really mean for us young people who grew up in a hyperconnected world?

With the rise of artificial intelligence and data analytics, platforms are learning more about us humans than they do. As you share every moment, from food dishes to your deepest thoughts (yes, even in those memes that seem so funny), you leave a digital trail that can be analyzed and used in ways you may not be aware of.

Self-taught education is the best option rather than mindlessly sliding through social networks, learning about how algorithms work, what filter bubbles are and how data is used. There are online resources, from tutorials to documentaries, that break down these concepts in language that simplifies understanding them. To become educated is to become empowered. The more you know, the more able you will be to make informed decisions about what you share and how you interact in the digital world.

On privacy. Every photo, post or share becomes valuable data that companies can sell. So adjusting who can see those posts or stopping access to unnecessary apps can make a big difference.

Building a community is critical. Making the topic of digital surveillance part of everyday conversations can be a game changer. Organizing chats at school or in groups of friends about experiences with online privacy not only helps with reflection, but also builds connections. Tips on how to protect data can be shared or news about personal privacy can be discussed.

The future of digital surveillance also has the opportunity to innovate, from social media campaigns to viral videos that explain how to protect privacy. Social platforms can be used to generate awareness, creating hashtags, posts or trends that draw the public's attention to privacy.

It is critical to recognize that there is also the ability to demand change in the realm of digital privacy. The voices of young people have proven to be extraordinarily influential, as evidenced in movements related to climate change, where coming together has led to leaders paying attention. It therefore raises the possibility of applying this same collective strength in the context of digital privacy. This can be achieved by signing petitions, participating in protests, and pressuring companies to act with greater transparency regarding the use of personal data.

Although the future of digital surveillance may seem complicated, you are not trapped in this situation. Through education, protecting privacy, making connections with others and demanding change, it is possible to transform this landscape. It is time to take control of the digital narrative and ensure that voices are heard in the world that is being built.

Bibliographic references

Altium (2024). Controlling the Future: 7 Trends in Industrial Control Systems. https://resources.altium.eom/es/p/controlling-future-7-trends-industrial-control-systems

Bartolomé, M. (2021). Social networks, disinformation, cyber sovereignty and digital surveillance: a view from cybersecurity. RESI: Journal of studies in international security, 7(2), 167-185. https://dialnet.unirioja.es/servlet/articulo?codigo=83Q6Q43

Carrasco Díaz-Masa, S. (2021). THE USE OF TECHNOLOGIES FOR SOCIAL CONTROL BY POWER GROUPS. SCIO: Revista De Filosofía, (20), 63-91. https://doi.org/1Q.46583/scio 2Q21.2Q.816

Cohen, J. E. (2012). Configuring the networked self: Law, code, and the play of everyday practice. Yale University Press. https://books.google.es/books?hl=es&lr=&id= FnQDjthDpsC&oi= fnd&pg=PP2&dq= Configuring+the+Networked+Self:+Law.+Code.+and+the+Play+of+Everyday+ Practi ce.&ots= xnCLvEcYDS&sig=z tOzcB5QnQhwVOzX8b7242Lf98.

Datos101. (n.d.). Digital Surveillance: How to Stay Ahead of Cybercriminals. https://www.datos1Q1.com/blog/vigilancia-digital/.

Fernández, P. (Ed.). (2017). *Big data: Eje estratégico en la industria audiovisual.* Editorial uoc. https://books.google.es/books?hl=es&lr=&id=WOc8DgAAQBAJ&oi=fnd&pg= PT3& dq=Big+data:+strategic+axis%C3%A9gico+in+the+audiovisual+industry.+&ots =PLdWwVbyfL&sig=BCdkntp1vaKgWSrMqETF YDT3Ck#v=onepage&q=Big%20data%3A %20eje%20estrat%20estrat%C3%A9gico%20en%20la%20industria%20audiovisual.&f=false

Foucault, M. (2002). *Vigilar y castigar: nacimiento de la prisión.* Siglo xxi. https://dialnet.unirioja.es/descarga/articulo/4899437.pdf

Foucault, M. (1980). *The eye of power. La piqueta. Spain.* *https://campusacademica.rec.uba.ar/pluginfile.php7file=%2F988701%2Fmodjfolder*

%2Fcontent%2F0%2FMICHEL%20FOUCAULT%20EL%20OJO%20DEL%20 DEL%20POD ER%7D.pdf&forcedownload=1

García y García, M. (2019). On the panopticon: Bentham, Foucault, and Han. Marginal Reflections, 50. apa citation to the author of this link: https://revista.reflexionesmarginales.com/sobre-el-panoptico-bentham-foucault-y-han/

Gutiérrez Zurdo, M. (2019). Foucault's panopticon in today's society: information and communication technologies. https://uvadoc.uva.es/bitstream/handle/10324/36903/TFG-N.1096.pdf?sequence=1

Han, B. C. (2024). In the swarm. Herder Editorial. https://books.google.es/books?hl=es&lr=&id=IFQCEQAAQBAJ&oi=fnd&pg=PT54&dq=El+swarm+Han&ots=2seSuBS4pd&sig=vuOR44Rj5Yx354X9JwHc k8GTDu M

Hortal, P. (2018). Transformation: technology and social control. Facthum. https://facthum.com/transformacion-tecnologia-y-control-social/

Lyon, D. (2016). As apostas de Snowden: desafios para entendimento de vigilância hoje. https://www.semanticscholar.org/paper/As-apostas-de-Snowden%3A-desafios-para-en tendimento-Lyon/adc5a21beaa211cbf6b2ec083c2ac5840403cc14e0.

Lyon, D. (2018). Review of Lyon's The Culture of Surveillance: Watching as a Way of Life. Surveillance & Society. https://www.semanticscholar.org/paper/The-culture-of-suiveillance%3A-watehing-as- a-way-of-Bryan/5172fcfe61b98c9e91e38e493dd527f2e9885422.

Marwick, A. E. (2013). Status update: Celebrity, publicity, and branding in the social media age. Yale University Press. https://books.google.es/books7hl=es&lr=&id=xcrYAQAAQBAJ&oi=fnd&pg=PA1&dq=info: EQvgZXcOQbwJ:scholar.google.com/&ots=G1lZTY2Y1S&sig=nPSD07fQaZJ y4v2u ZQ5Twq5iyGc#v=onepage&q&f=false.

OSHA (2022). Control Technologies: The Quest for 21st Century Well-Being. osha.europa.eu/es/themes/monitoring-technology-21st-centurys-pursui t-wellbeing.

World Health Organization (WHO). (2024). Ethics of public health surveillance. https://www.who.int/es/news-room/questions-and-answers/item/q-a-ethics-in-public-h ealth-surveillance.

Pan American Health Organization (PAHO). (2017). Information and communication technologies in the training of human resources for health: Innovative experiences in Latin America and the Caribbean. Washington, D.C.: PAHO. https://iris.paho.org/bitstream/handle/10665.2/34499/9789275319840-spa.pdf.

Pariser, E. (2011). The filter bubble: What the internet is hiding from you. Penguin Press. https://books.google.es/books7hl=es&lr=&id=-FWO0puw3nYC&oi=fnd&pg=PT24&dq=info:wgpXIqrJMsEJ:scholar.google.com/&ots=g6JoCpyPQZ&sig=B7N2wuqdSd9 w0PrLndE SjQvx-s#v=onepage&q&f=false

Ramonet, I., Assange, J., Chomsky, N., & Sacristán, M. (2016). *El imperio de la vigilancia.* Madrid: Clave intelectual. https://www.eldiplo.org/wp-content/uploads/2018/files/7114/6040/1796/INTRODUC CION.pdf.

Regan, P.M. (1995). Legislating Privacy: Technology, Social Values, and Public Policy. The Handbook of Privacy Studies. https://www.semanticscholar.org/paper/Legislating-Privacy%3A-Technology%2C-Soc ial-Values%2C-and-Regan/bcb4dcd6f427c845880a183ddb58fd860b8448c8

Rubio, C. A. (2020). The social network Facebook as a control device. A look from Foucault's philosophy. *Sincronía,* (77), 165-180. https://www.redalyc.org/journal/5138/513862147008/html/

Turkle, S. (2011). Alone together: Why we expect more from technology and less from each other. Basic Books. https://www.semanticscholar.org/paper/Alone-Together%3A-Why-We-Expect-More-f rom-Technology-Turkle/57f3a16a88d74fbd4873112177228a21309f001f.

Zuboff, S. (2020). *The age of surveillance capitalism: The struggle for a humane future at the new frontier of power.* http ://d.d.org/10.1007 /s001-020 -01100 -0.

Printed by Books on Demand GmbH, Norderstedt / Germany